Meet the Minibeasts

Invertebrates on the GROUND

by
Rebecca Phillips-Bartlett

Minneapolis, Minnesota

Credits

All images are courtesy of Shutterstock.com, unless otherwise specified. With thanks to Getty Images, Thinkstock Photo, and iStockphoto. Recurring images – Guz Anna, TWINS DESIGN STUDIO, Bulgakova Christina, ebi_ko, Rawpixel.com. Cover – irin-k, Aleksandar Dickov, Eric Isselee, andregric, Zuzha. 2–3 – mehmetkrc. 4–5 – Adil Celebiyev StokPhoto, Shaplov Evgeny. 6–7 – Zebra-Studio, Bozhena Melnyk. 8–9 – Azmil Umry, Dmytro Khlystun. 10–11 – Anatolir, Anna-Nas, Tomas Vacek. 12–13 – PinkPueblo, natchapohn, Mark Brandon, frank60, AspctStyle. 14–15 – K Hanley CHDPhoto, Park Ji Sun, Sukarman. 16–17 – HHelene, Keroro. 18–19 – YoONSpY, Yuangeng Zhang. 20–21 – Ezume Images, Milton Buzon, Nutkins.J. 22–23 – BushAlex, JGA.

Bearport Publishing Company Product Development Team

Publisher: Jen Jenson; Director of Product Development: Spencer Brinker; Managing Editor: Allison Juda; Editor: Cole Nelson; Associate Editor: Naomi Reich; Associate Editor: Tiana Tran; Designer: Kim Jones; Designer: Kayla Eggert; Designer: Steve Scheluchin; Production Specialist: Owen Hamlin

Library of Congress Cataloging-in-Publication Data is available at www.loc.gov or upon request from the publisher.

ISBN: 979-8-89577-020-7 (hardcover)
ISBN: 979-8-89577-451-9 (paperback)
ISBN: 979-8-89577-137-2 (ebook)

© 2026 BookLife Publishing
This edition is published by arrangement with BookLife Publishing.

North American adaptations © 2026 Bearport Publishing Company. All rights reserved. No part of this publication may be reproduced in whole or in part, stored in any retrieval system, or transmitted in any form or by any means, electronic, mechanical, photocopying, recording, or otherwise, without written permission from the publisher. Bearport Publishing is a division of FlutterBee Education Group.

For more information, write to Bearport Publishing, 5357 Penn Avenue South, Minneapolis, MN 55419.

CONTENTS

Minibeasts on the Ground 4

Snails 6

Grasshoppers 8

Spiders 10

Stick Insects 12

Caterpillars 14

Beetles 16

Mantises 18

Millipedes 20

So Many Minibeasts 22

Glossary 24

Index 24

MINIBEASTS
ON THE GROUND

Hi there! My name is Harry Hedgehog. I dig around for food here on the forest floor. I eat mostly small **invertebrates**, such as **insects** and spiders.

An invertebrate is an animal with no backbone.

I like calling these small and tasty animals minibeasts. I share my forest **habitat** with lots of minibeasts. They are my favorite foods!

Are you ready to meet some minibeasts?

SNAILS

Snails stand out from many other minibeasts thanks to their shells. Snails use shells to stay safe and to hide from **predators**.

Shells are tough to chew!

A snail's shell is its own tiny home.

6

Snails move around by using a long foot on the bottom of their bodies. They often leave trails of slime behind them. This sticky slime helps snails climb up plants to get food.

FACT FILE

Size: Up to 2 inches (5 cm) long

Diet: Leaves, vegetables, and flowers

Habitat: Forests, fields, and wetlands

GRASSHOPPERS

What is that sound coming from the grass? It's a grasshopper! Grasshoppers are loud minibeasts. They make sounds by rubbing their legs on their wings.

Many grasshoppers are green like the grass. This helps them hide.

Grasshoppers are crunchy and yummy!

Like many insects, grasshoppers have wings. But they also have very strong back legs. They can jump high and then fly even farther. Some grasshoppers can jump up to 30 in. (76 cm) in one leap.

FACT FILE

Size: Up to 2.7 in. (7 cm) long
Diet: Leaves, flowers, and seeds
Habitat: Fields and grasslands

SPIDERS

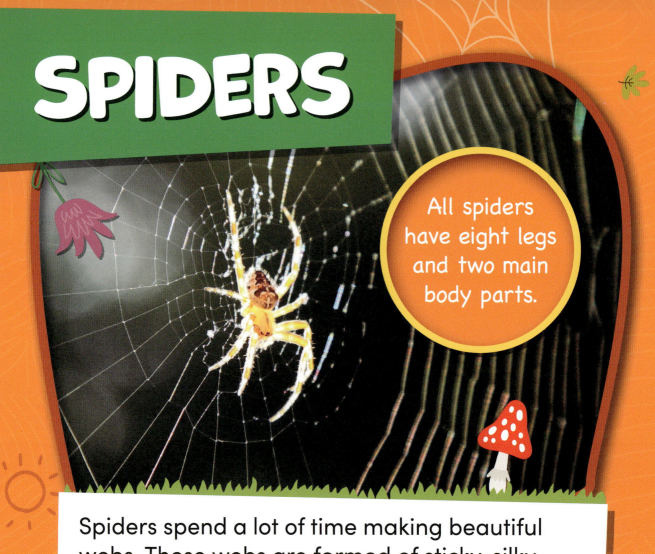

All spiders have eight legs and two main body parts.

Spiders spend a lot of time making beautiful webs. These webs are formed of sticky, silky threads that spiders make in their bodies. Many spiders use these webs to catch their **prey**.

Most spiders are harmless to humans. In fact, they are often helpful. Spiders protect gardens by catching insects that eat plants.

FACT FILE

Size: Up to 5 in. (12.7 cm) long

Diet: Insects

Habitat: Everywhere except Antarctica

STICK INSECTS

Stick insects are good at hiding from predators. They use **camouflage** to look like the sticks and leaves where they live.

Can you spot the stick insect?

This insect has a clever way of surviving an attack. If a predator catches one of its legs, the stick insect can break it off to escape. It can then regrow the leg later.

Stick insects are the longest insects on Earth.

FACT FILE

Size: Up to 22 in. (55 cm) long
Diet: Leaves
Habitat: Forests and grasslands

13

CATERPILLARS

Butterflies and moths start their lives as caterpillars. Caterpillars need to eat lots of leaves to grow. They spend up to three weeks eating.

As caterpillars get bigger, they **molt** and grow new skin.

Once a caterpillar has grown big enough, it makes a case to protect itself. Soon, it comes out of the case as a butterfly or moth.

A chrysalis

Moth caterpillars make a silky case called a cocoon. Butterfly caterpillars turn into a chrysalis with a tough case.

FACT FILE

Size: Up to 4.5 in. (11.5 cm) long

Diet: Plants and leaves

Habitat: Forests, fields, and wetlands

BEETLES

All adult beetles have two sets of wings. Their hard top wings protect their lower wings. While most beetles can fly, many spend a lot of their time digging in the ground for food.

Top wings

Lower wings

16

Beetles cannot see very well. Instead, they learn about their surroundings by using their antennae. Their antennae pick up smells in the air. They can also use them to taste food.

Antennae

FACT FILE

Size: Up to 7.5 in. (19 cm) long

Diet: Plants, insects, tadpoles, dung, and small fish

Habitat: Everywhere except Antarctica and high mountains

Some beetles help move **pollen** between flowers so the plants can grow.

MANTISES

Mantises are great hunters. These insects often hunt other minibeasts that share their habitat. Mantises have sharp, spiky legs that help them hold onto their prey.

Mantises have eyes that can look both forward and backward.

Mantises are very good at using camouflage to hide. Many mantises are green to blend in with leaves. However, some are more colorful and look like flowers.

FACT FILE

Size: Up to 18 in. (45 cm) long

Diet: Insects, spiders, and small reptiles or birds

Habitat: Grasslands with lots of plants

MILLIPEDES

Millipedes have been on Earth longer than most animals!

The name *millipede* means a thousand feet. However, most millipedes actually have only a few hundred feet. Still, that's a lot!

A millipede's body is made of many sections. Each is covered in a hard shell. A hard covering like this is called an **exoskeleton**.

FACT FILE

Size: Up to 5 in. (13 cm) long
Diet: Mostly dead plants
Habitat: Areas with moist soil

SO MANY MINIBEASTS

The ground is home to lots of minibeasts. Many of these animals have very important jobs. Some spread pollen, while others protect plants from hungry insects.

There are so many creatures right beneath your feet. When you go outside, take a closer look at the ground. What do you see?

What is your favorite minibeast on the ground?

GLOSSARY

camouflage coloring that makes animals look like their surroundings

exoskeleton the hard covering that protects the body of some animals

habitat a place in nature where a plant or animal normally lives

insects small animals that have six legs, an exoskeleton, two antennae, and three main body parts

invertebrates animals that don't have backbones

molt to shed an outer layer

pollen a dust made by flowers that helps them make new plants

predators animals that hunt and eat other animals

prey an animal that is hunted by other animals for food

INDEX

antennae 17

camouflage 12, 19

exoskeletons 21

leaves 7, 9, 12–15, 19

legs 8–10, 13, 18

plants 7, 11–12, 15, 17, 19, 21–22

prey 10, 18

shells 6–7, 21

wings 8–9, 16